EXPLODING TURKEYS AND SPARE TROUSERS

ADVENTURES IN GLOBAL BUSINESS

KEN PASTERNAK

T0273037

First published in Great Britain by Practical Inspiration Publishing, 2021

© Ken Pasternak, 2021

The moral rights of the author have been asserted.

ISBN 9781788602815 (print)
9781788602808 (epub)
9781788602792 (mobi)

Practical Inspiration
Publishing

Endorsements for *Exploding Turkeys and Spare Trousers*

'Inspiring! *Exploding Turkeys and Spare Trousers* utilizes short, often humorous stories to pack profound truths and insights from Ken Pasternak's tales from around the world and throughout his career. A great read for the fundamentals of business!'

– Marshall Goldsmith, New York Times #1 bestselling author of *Triggers, Mojo,* and *What Got You Here Won't Get You There*

'As a fellow road warrior, I fully appreciate Ken's creative and insightful work. His stories are poignant, entertaining, and authentic, and his insights captivating. The work lets everyone experience being a road warrior without being on the road!'

– Dave Ulrich, Rensis Likert Professor, Ross School of Business, University of Michigan

'Ken is a wonderful storyteller with an uncanny ability to just capture that telling moment that everyone will delight in reading. I could not manage to put the book down.'

– René Carayol MBE, author and leading executive coach

'The content of this book is as intriguing as its title – many descriptions of real-life experiences from one of the most travelled individuals I know. Congrats to Ken for a great job; there is nothing more telling than stories. This is a must read.'

– Fons Trompenaars, world-renowned expert on international management and author of the global bestseller *Riding the Waves of Culture*

'Ken's global career inspired these life lessons and colorfully presented leadership precepts. With clever humor combined with common sense, he delivers wisdom that enriches and enlightens the reader. Explore the world while sampling bite-sized morsels from every delicious page.'

– Barbara M. Barrett, US Secretary of the Air Force (2019–21) and US Ambassador to Finland (2008–09)

'I've known Ken since his early research into how Formula 1 teams achieve high performance and extreme innovation. Just as F1 operates across the globe, Ken's stories highlight his experiences doing business in different cultures. This book includes a few F1-related stories and much, much more. A great read while sitting on an airplane or anytime.'

– Ross Brawn, Managing Director of Motor Sports, Formula 1

'This superbly crafted book at first glance seems to be a collection of 53 vignettes about Ken's work and travels over a fascinating globe-trotting career. But the lessons and takeaways offer a managerial tapestry that can be useful in a reader's business or personal life. Read one story at a time; mix and match them. Useful insight is guaranteed from this superbly written book.'

– George McGurn, Egremont Board of Selectmen, and Dean Emeritus, Boston University School of Management

'Ken Pasternak shares incredibly inspiring true stories with universal leadership lessons, touching humanness at the core. He shows how business life can become a deeper journey of inner growth when we are open, present, curious, in the moment, flexible, always ready to help out a friend or a stranger, and take a chance at what life offers. A timeless book on what true, masterful leadership is all about.'

– Nicole Heimann, Co-CEO, Executive Coach and Executive Team Coach at Heimann Cvetkovic & Partners AG and author of *How to Develop the Authentic Leader in You*

'In this excellent book, Ken Pasternak offers incredibly valuable practical leadership lessons wrapped into vivid stories. His tales are insightful, amusing, and sometimes surprising. In all cases, the reader is rewarded with a takeaway that can be useful for becoming a better leader and a better person.'

– Dr. Oleg Konovalov, bestselling author of *The Vision Code*

'The power of storytelling is seriously underestimated, particularly when relating real personal experiences. Ken adeptly draws deep insights from these personal encounters, making them all the more compelling.'

**– John McFarlane OBE, Chairman,
Westpac Banking Corporation**

'Ken Pasternak shares his international business experience and storytelling skills in a book that informs, educates, and entertains. His short stories cover a wide range of situations from which executives and business school students will derive useful takeaways for developing their own leadership and team-building capabilities.'

**– John A. Quelch CBE, Vice Provost, University of
Miami, Dean, Miami Herbert Business School
and Leonard M. Miller University Professor**

'Storytelling makes events come alive. Ken's book is a great collection of stories about international business. At a time of increasing cynicism, Ken's stories show how people, friendship, and empathy also have their place in business. Truly enjoyable!'

**– Pekka Pohjakallio, Director, Global Business
Development and Executive Mentor,
Hintsa Performance**

'Ken Pasternak takes his readers on a journey of discovery and knowledge into global business where through storytelling he cleverly, eloquently, and generously provides his subtle leadership, personal and professional insights. I highly recommend this book.'

**– Dr. Abraham Khoureis, university professor and the
host of podcast *Leadership & Politics with Dr. Abraham***

'Ken is a world-class leader, mentor, teacher, speaker, and writer. He has tremendous wisdom, and when he shares it you can tell he's reflected carefully based on his vast experiences. Don't miss the opportunity to live vicariously and learn through Ken's global adventures.'

**— Bonnie Hagemann, CEO,
Executive Development Associates, Inc.**

'Through powerful anecdotes and lively storytelling, this book unveils the hard-learned and invaluable lessons from Ken Pasternak's professional life and career. It is filled with fresh insights and personal experiences, as well as offering thoughtful and pragmatic lessons to which readers from students to CEOs will relate and that they will find useful in both their business activities and in life generally. Ken offers wisdom and the gift of much-needed common sense, chapter by chapter and experience by experience. I recommend this book highly for anyone who wants to gain valuable insights from a consummate storyteller. A must-read!'

— Professor Sattar Bawany, CEO, Disruptive Leadership Institute, Professor of Practice, IPE Management School, Paris and author of *Leadership in Disruptive Times*

'Ken Pasternak has prepared a spicy gumbo of great advice and thoughtful observations, served in entertaining and memorable bites. From alliances to attitude, culture to communications, there's something useful and informative for every taste.'

— Mary Jo Jacobi, strategic advisor, corporate director, broadcast commentator and public speaker

'Ken takes readers into his amazing life journey, sharing personal and professional experiences that bring valuable insights applicable to anyone's life. From navigating challenging business situations to cultural awakenings, he draws key learnings from organizations, businesses, and teams. Regardless of the reader's location or line of business, every page and every story is a treasure.'

— Horace O. Porrás, Vice President, Human Resources, American Tower Corporation

'Ken Pasternak's collection of short stories is a fresh take on a business and leadership book. He shares insightful observations about leadership, teamwork, and human behavior, perceptively and often humorously. Readers will gain new perspectives, whether they pick up the book just for a few minutes or take more time with it. Ken's anecdotes are a reminder about how small moments can offer important learnings.'

– Satu Huber, Former Chief Executive Officer, Elo Mutual Pension Insurance Company

'Insightful, refreshing, and fun stories shared in an easily relatable way that helps us reflect on key learnings that arise out of situations in our lives.'

– Alberto Carrero, Senior Executive Coach and Partner, Inside Out

Contents

Introduction

On a recent video call with friends, the discussion revolved around how much each of us values the storytelling that happens when people get together – perhaps now, in a post-pandemic world, more than ever.

In almost five decades of managing, teaching, and consulting, storytelling has – for me at least – been a vital means of communication. A well-constructed tale has enabled me to deliver key messages on the job and during personal encounters, especially when communicating across diverse cultures. People are more likely to retain an important lesson when it is attached to a compelling story, be it serious, humorous, or just plain fun.

I have been very fortunate to travel extensively around the world, working for two international organizations, and during the past 24 years as a consultant, teacher, and keynote speaker. I was working in Hungary before the fall of the Berlin Wall; advising in China already in 1988; building a teaching institution in Turkey when there was only one, not three, bridges across the Bosporus; traveling across Russia just as the Soviet Union was dissolved; visiting South Sudan soon after its independence; and in recent times helping a variety of organizations improve their leadership and teamwork capabilities while developing agile mindsets and building high-performance cultures.

A while ago, I began recording these experiences as stories to share on LinkedIn. At the outset, I did not know that a post was limited to only 1300 characters, or about 200 words, and while at first I found this an annoying constraint, I discovered that it forced me to describe my remembrances as concisely as possible. I also learned that many readers want stories and messages delivered in an easily digestible format. This book is the result of those posts. It contains some of the stories I published on LinkedIn and many more. While I have chosen to liberate myself from LinkedIn's 1300-character restriction for the stories in this book, the lessons I have learned about brevity and digestibility remain.

Much of my career has been spent offering pragmatic advice to executives, aiming to help them, as leaders, to improve their own and their organization's performance. With this in mind, I have added an observation or lesson at the end of each story. My hope is that you will find these thought-provoking and useful as you consider your work situation or personal life.

The book is divided into seven chapters: Leadership; Working with others; Timing is everything; Communications; Cultural encounters; Business perspectives; and Personal observations. The stories in each chapter are tied together by their key takeaways.

The stories are short so they can be read in any manner you wish – the whole book, from front to back, following the thread in a specific section, or dipping in and out.

I hope these stories provide you with enjoyable and useful observations that are relevant and helpful in your business and personal life.

We are always learning.

Ken Pasternak, Helsinki, Finland

1

Leadership

Lateral thinking

In 1975, I was a young corporate banker in New York City. For one bankrupt client, I attended court proceedings and sat on the senior creditors' committee. Emerging from that failed discount store chain was a company called Toys R Us. Banks were vying to be its lead financial institution.

We had expertise in that industry, but one creative idea might have sealed the outcome in our favor.

We often received requests from senior executives for charitable donations to causes they supported. These were sent to a corporate department that handled such items. After Toys R Us emerged, we received one such request from the company's founder and President, Charles Lazarus, who was being honored as 'Toy Man of the Year' at a Plaza Hotel charity dinner.

I shared the request with my boss, who asked me, 'If we buy a table and take this as a marketing expense, can we fill it with the company's senior executives?' I replied, 'Sure!' with youthful confidence.

We did fill the table and were the only bankers attending the event. A few days later, I was summoned to a meeting at the company's headquarters and we were awarded financing of its international toy imports and other banking needs.

Did our attendance at the charity event make a difference? I will never know for sure, but my boss's imaginative, lateral thinking made a lasting impression on me.

Empathy

It was 1979 in New York. I was broadening my banking knowledge by attending a five-day seminar on real estate lending. It covered the pitfalls and methods of lending to a very risky industry. We discussed two case studies each day; however, one session stood out for me.

In this case study, we had to determine the protagonist's motivation and understand his actions. Was he unscrupulous or honorable; callous or sympathetic?

After discussing the case study in small teams, the plenary session was lively. Everyone decided that the central character was a villain of the worst sort. We laid into him for the manipulative ways in which he operated. Out loud, he was called a 'f**king a**h*le,' among other choice names.

The instructor started his wrap-up and asked us to turn around. Pointing to a man sitting in the back of the room, he said, 'I would like to introduce you to the 'f**king a**h*le' you have been talking about.' Our jaws dropped. We had not noticed him and would not have known who he was even if we had.

He walked to the front and shared the facts and situation as he had seen and lived it. He explained what he did and why. We began to see him in quite a different light. It was a great teaching device and learning experience.

The experience helped me realize that we do not truly know someone until we have walked in their shoes and seen the situation from their point of view.

Heroes

In my experience, employees focus their attention mainly on two leaders in the organization: their immediate supervisor and the CEO. I have often found it is important to remind executives that they are being watched *all the time* by their employees, peers, and other stakeholders.

How a leader behaves sets the tone for the whole organization and strongly influences its culture.

August 2020 was the 25th anniversary of the death of one of my boyhood idols, Mickey Mantle. 'The Mick' was a baseball player for the New York Yankees in the 1950s and 1960s – an American icon.

He was a leader on the field, but throughout his life never considered himself a role model and never wanted to be one. Even so, he was a hero to young boys who imitated him and adult men who wished they were him.

I recall seeing the front-page news of his death while reading the *International Herald Tribune* on August 13, 1995. It spontaneously brought tears to my eyes. Like many heroes, he was flawed, but that did not lessen my feeling of loss or reduce the influence he had had on me.

Leaders at all levels of an organization do not necessarily aspire to be heroes, but they must remember that their actions *always* influence the behavior of others.

Leaders are 'on stage' all the time, and are role models whether they want to be or not.

Playing for my high school basketball team —
taking a shot or passing?

Leadership style

'Envisioning' is conceiving or seeing something in one's mind.

Playing tennis, I envision hitting a topspin backhand like Roger Federer. The reality may be different, but creating and trying to emulate a mental image is a proven tool for improving sports performance.

In 1984, I was attending an intense, in-company 'Managing People' program in Frankfurt with case studies, role-plays and exercises. It also included anonymous feedback from my team members and comparisons of my scores to a database of past course participants.

A personal coach guided each of us through the insightful results and offered advice.

In one counselling session, he asked, 'What kind of leader do you want to be?' I had no answer. He then asked whether I had played any team sports. I said I loved playing basketball.

He told me to envision playing basketball and focus on my role in the team. I described my preferred position as point guard, passing and creating scoring opportunities for my teammates. 'Did you not also try to shoot?' he asked. I replied, 'Sure I did, but I got greater enjoyment from setting up someone else to score.'

It was a revelation for me about my leadership philosophy and my personal leadership style.

President Harry Truman is said to have commented, 'It is amazing what you can accomplish if you do not care who gets the credit.'

With Dan Rather and Dominique Strauss-Kahn at the Joint Vienna Institute

Hubris

In late 2010, I was in Austria teaching a course to leaders of small and medium enterprises from Eastern Europe at the Joint Vienna Institute.

The Managing Director of the International Monetary Fund (IMF), Dominique Strauss-Kahn, stopped by to speak to the group. He was being shadowed by Dan Rather, a famous American television journalist who was making a documentary about him. Strauss-Kahn spoke knowledgably to the group about issues important to the participants and discussed actions taken by the international financial community to support economic development in their countries.

At the time, Strauss-Kahn was a very well-respected leader, and by early 2011 many even thought he could be a viable challenger to become France's next president. However, in May 2011 he abruptly resigned from the IMF in the wake of allegations that he had shown poor judgment and unacceptable behaviors in his personal life.

This is not the first time we have seen leaders fall from great heights, but when it happens we are still shocked and dismayed.

We want to follow leaders who demonstrate self-confidence, but when they display arrogance and act outside acceptable societal norms, it is only right that they are called out. There are numerous examples in government and industry where leaders have behaved in ways that were not consistent with the values they espoused for their organizations. Thinking themselves exempt from the very principles they expect others to follow has rightfully led to their eventual downfall.

There is no place in leadership for hubris.

British Grand Prix Formula 1 paddock area at Silverstone race circuit

Presence

Over the past 15 years, I have been fortunate to attend Formula 1 Grand Prix events around the world. In July 2019, I was at the Silverstone racetrack in the United Kingdom attending the British Grand Prix. I was lucky enough to gain admittance into the Paddock, an exclusive area where one can meet drivers and team leaders, and enter remarkable two- to three-story motorhomes housing restaurants, meeting rooms, and offices.

There are also chance encounters with celebrities who are there to plug a project, or just to be seen. I never take entrance into this unique world for granted, but last year I was caught off-guard by one celebrity sighting. Entering one of the motorhomes for a meeting with a journalist, I passed the first row of tables and recognized an all-time favorite of mine, the 'real' 007, Sean Connery. He was seated on his own, then was joined by his wife carrying their lunch on a tray.

I wanted to approach him but could tell from the 'leave me alone' look on his face that a handshake or (heaven forbid!) a selfie would be out of the question. Looking around the room, it seemed that proper etiquette meant one should act as if he were not there. While talking with the journalist, I sat with my back to Mr. Connery, lest I spend the entire time watching him eat.

I was impressed with the restraint shown by everyone in the room, offering this well-known personality space and relative privacy. Without exchanging a word, sitting just a few feet from a cinema hero, I could feel his presence.

Some leaders, like some celebrities, exude a sense of presence just by being in the room.

2

Working with others

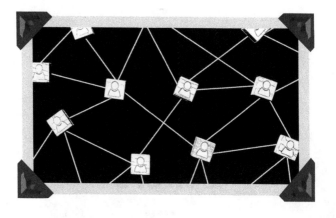

Networking

Networking is important. By this I mean not just handing out business cards or finding 'friends' on social media; the value of true networking lies in establishing and nurturing relationships where giving and receiving support happens in equal measure.

In 1988, I was in Budapest advising the Central Bank of Hungary on the establishment of what would become the first training center for bankers in Central and Eastern Europe. Hungarian Prime Minister Miklos Nemeth spoke at the Institute's opening ceremony, and afterward he and I talked about developing the country's financial sector.

Fast forward to early 1996. I had been working for four years at the European Bank for Reconstruction and Development (EBRD) in London. My team was helping to establish banking and business teaching institutions throughout Eastern Europe and the Commonwealth of Independent States. A new president at the EBRD was making significant changes. I learned that my department would likely be closed, so I proposed outsourcing the team. This would allow us to continue delivering our outstanding projects and meet the president's budgetary goals. I would in effect become a consultant to the EBRD. Several members of my team would remain, reporting to me, supervising projects until their conclusion before being transferred to new assignments. The rest of my team would be redeployed to other positions in the bank.

To accomplish this redesign, I needed the approval of the Head of Human Resources, Miklos Nemeth. We had met from time to time since our first meeting, and he was aware of my team's accomplishments. That track record — and perhaps our personal association in Hungary eight years earlier — provided background for him to support my proposal.

The outsourcing successfully delivered results for the EBRD and started me on my career as a consultant.

Like friendships, networks and relationships can exist for a reason, a season, and if we are lucky, for life.

Recognition

'You've made my day!' It is so gratifying when someone says that to you.

In 2006, my wife and I were invited to attend a reception at Buckingham Palace in support of the National Youth Theater. The event was hosted by Prince Edward, the Earl of Wessex, but this story is not about him. It is about a different kind of British royalty: *comedy* royalty. At the event I met Ronnie Corbett, CBE – all 5 feet of him! Corbett was a legend in Britain, starting from his comedy sketch shows on the BBC in the 1960s.

During cocktails, I asked whether he knew how important he was to business students around the world. At first, he did now know what I was talking about. Then I reminded him that in the 1970s he had made a series of business training films with John Cleese, of Monty Python fame. The videos explained financial accounting concepts – balance sheets, income statements and working capital – with clarity and a sense of humor. It made my job of teaching the subject to international course participants at Citibank's European Training Centre in London much easier.

I thanked him for that.

He, in turn, thanked me for telling him about the contribution those videos had made.

We clinked our glasses, and I must admit it felt wonderful to hear him say, 'You've made my day!'

Jordan Racing Team motorhome at Imola
race circuit, Italy

Look into my eyes

Are our eyes the windows to the soul?

I attended my first Formula 1 Grand Prix in 2004. My co-authors and I were at the Imola race circuit in Italy, holding very precious paddock passes. These gave us behind-the-scenes access to the teams' motorhomes so we could conduct interviews for the first edition of *Performance at the Limit: Business Lessons from Formula 1 Racing.*

In the modest Jordan Grand Prix Racing facility, we were recording a conversation with Team Principal Eddie Jordan. Legendary driver Michael Schumacher had made his F1 debut on Jordan's team in 1991. That led me to ask him, 'How can you tell whether a young driver has what it takes to succeed in F1?'

We were seated next to each other on a banquette. Jordan's goateed face leaned in extremely close to mine, he stared unblinkingly into my eyes, slowly moved even closer and emphatically said, 'I look into their $@%#ing eyes to see if they have the $@%#ing desire and $@%#ing stamina to succeed in this $@%#ing sport!'

My co-authors still enjoy recounting how stunned and over-whelmed I was as I struggled not to fall to the floor.

Maybe the eyes are the portal to one's soul. Given Schumacher's seven Driver World Championships, Jordan certainly must have seen something special in him.

On the other hand, upon looking into my eyes, Jordan knew instantly that I was better off writing about race cars than driving them!

When communicating, extended eye contact is considered important in many cultures, but not in all. One should be aware of what is appropriate behavior, depending on your environment and situation.

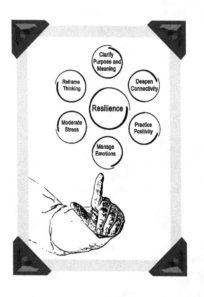

Resilience

The European Bank for Reconstruction and Development (EBRD) was founded in London in 1991. When I joined in March 1992, we were in temporary offices prior to the completion of our new Broadgate headquarters.

I returned to London from a trip to Kiev late on Friday night, April 10, 1992. The next morning, I got up early and headed to the office to catch up on work and write my trip report. Climbing the stairs from Bank Underground Station, I saw a dozen police cars and yellow tape cordoning off the area. They forbade me from going further and ordered me to return home.

I did not know that on the previous day the Provisional IRA had detonated a one-ton bomb at the nearby Baltic Exchange, causing £800 million in damage to that building and many others, including ours. Three people were killed and 91 injured.

A week later, we were allowed back into our office to collect personal items and files. The windows were blown out and glass was strewn everywhere.

For several weeks, we worked from apartments and hotel rooms using the only technology available at the time – landline phones, faxes, and patchy emails.

What I remember most was how our team pulled together during the crisis. We supported each other and maintained momentum under challenging circumstances during the EBRD's formative days.

You cannot teach resilience. It comes from dedicated people sharing a vision, believing in a mission, and maintaining a can-do attitude.

Speaking at the EFMD Conference for Deans and
Directors of business schools, Koç University, Istanbul

Attitude

In 2013, I delivered a keynote address at the European Foundation for Management Development conference at Koç University in Istanbul. In the audience were 200 deans from international business schools. My assigned topic was, 'What will employers be looking for from MBA graduates five years from now?'

My basic premise was that to succeed in the workforce, technical competence acquired in business school was not the main issue. Rather, there needed to be more emphasis put on interpersonal, communication and teamworking skills. I stressed that those capabilities would increasingly be in demand as organizations strived to connect with more demanding customers, along with the subsequent need to work more effectively across internal functional silos.

I emphasized that organizations needed to have a clear sense of the fundamental beliefs on which they stood, and that they should seek employees whose values were in alignment with their own.

I reassured the audience that analytical skills would always be needed; however, employers would be hiring on the basis of a candidate's attitude. Corporate recruiters do not always know what future skills their companies will need, but they do know the fundamental mindset of the people they want.

I believe even more strongly now that people skills and attitude are keys to success in business life.

Alliances

The term 'strategic alliance' sounds positive and promising. Two companies, pooling resources for mutual benefit, while remaining independent.

In 1988, I joined a group within Citibank that provided consulting services to other financial institutions. We had offices in New York, Bogota, and Manila; and I opened one in Brussels.

A year later, we entered an alliance with a consulting business positioned within a global accounting firm. I travelled across Europe, getting to know our new partners, attending conferences to build relationships, and trying to source joint assignments.

Alas, except for one project in Spain, not much came of this venture in Europe – or anywhere else for that matter. We encountered some of the obstacles that crop up when organizations try to combine resources:

1. Our corporate cultures were different in many ways.
2. They had internal issues related to how consulting activities fit alongside a predominant accounting business.
3. As a corporation operating globally, country borders and internal profit center issues never got in the way of our meeting a customer's need. However, they were a collection of national partnerships, which did not take kindly to other parts of their organization playing in their domestic sandbox.

Corporate alliances, in any form, are challenging, and culture always plays a crucial role in their chances of success.

3

Timing is everything

Serendipity

One day I was walking to an important meeting near my home when it rained hard with strong, gusty winds. My umbrella was of no use, so my khaki trousers were soaked. I passed a second-hand clothing store — you probably know the kind. They have receptacles placed around the city for clothing donations. These items are sorted at a central facility and then distributed, in this case to one of their 12 stores around Helsinki.

I entered the store and on a small rack found a pair of khaki trousers. The label indicated a waist size and length that I knew would fit. What luck! Without trying them on I paid and ran to the meeting venue where, in the men's room, I put on the new trousers. It was a good meeting.

The rain had stopped when I walked home. Entering our home, my wife said, 'I thought you'd be more wet than this.' So I proudly shared my good fortune at the clothing store. She asked how much I had paid. I told her. She looked at me and burst out laughing. 'Do you realize that you just paid €13 for the trousers you donated a month ago?' I could not believe it. I slipped them off right there in our hallway for a closer inspection. Sure enough, it was true.

You may not always end up where you thought you were going, but you will always end up where you were meant to be. Apparently, the same is true for donated trousers.

Right timing

In October 2012, I was in Juba, South Sudan. It was a year after it became the world's newest country. My mission was to explore establishing a National Development Bank in support of the country's huge infrastructure need. Upon my arrival at the airport, a local television crew interviewed me about the project. This would be an interesting week.

I met government officials and presidential advisors, and delivered a presentation to members of parliament. After a week, in the airport departure lounge, I gave one last interview where I was conscious about the need to speak carefully to manage rising expectations. A few days later in Nairobi, I also met South Sudan's first vice president and gained his support for the project concept.

I began to assemble a team of experienced development bankers, designed a strategy to raise capital investments, and created a preliminary implementation plan. However, the project was not to be. In late 2013, South Sudan was engulfed in a civil war that lasted until early 2020.

In 2019, with hostilities in the country winding down and discussions of a unity government being formed, I was again contacted and asked to restart the Development Bank project. It had been seven years since my previous visit, so the team I had assembled was no longer available. All, like myself, had moved on to other opportunities that were taking 100% of our attention. I had to decline their request.

Often in life the opportunities we are offered and choices we must make are all about the right timing.

A portion of my collection of soccer figurines and memorabilia

Fate

Helsinki, November 2003. Entering the room late, I saw only one seat at a small table far from the guest speaker, Henry Kissinger. I remember that his remarks included the now famous question, 'Who do I call if I want to speak to Europe?'

After he finished speaking, introductions were made at our table. Across from me was a senior officer in the Finnish Ministry of Defence. We began with small talk, but this time it took a different turn than it normally would. Unusually for a Finn of his generation, he had received a university degree in the United States.

Me: Where?
Him: Harvard. I graduated 1973.
Me: I graduated from Yale that year. Did you do any extracurricular activities?
Him: Freshman year I was a fullback on the soccer team.
Me: No way! I was goalkeeper on the Yale team.

We realized that 30 years earlier, on a cold, windy field in Cambridge, Massachusetts, we had played against each other. He even recalled that Harvard won.

Soon after this chance meeting, we started a sauna/dinner group with business executives, military officers, and foreign ambassadors that met monthly. It was a unique and fun opportunity to engage in wide-ranging, off-the-record discussions. The group disbanded after eight years, but many close friendships have remained.

If I had not been late and found that one seat, none of this would have happened.

Truly, a stranger is a friend you haven't met yet!

The painting that caused commotion at Sheremetyevo Airport, purchased at an outdoor art market next to Gorky Park, Moscow

Good deed

In 1994, my wife joined me on a trip to Moscow. She and a Finnish friend living there toured the city while I was at meetings. At our hotel that evening, she showed me two purchases: an old wooden frame with intricate carvings and a recently completed oil painting of a scene in Karelia, purchased at a street market.

She was returning to London before me, so we put the frame in her suitcase. She would carry the painting, wrapped in brown paper, on the plane. At Sheremetyevo Airport, I watched while the customs officials gestured at her and raised their voices, claiming the painting was an antique and needed an export license. She objected and there was quite a to-do. I had to retrieve the painting so she would be allowed to continue to her flight back to London.

When her plane was in the air, an attendant brought her champagne and said it was compliments of two gentlemen in business class. Eventually, one came back and said, 'We are geologists and always have problems taking samples out of Russia, but because of the big commotion you caused at customs, they let us through without a problem. Thank you! And can we hire you?'

Later that week, I paid for an export license from the Ministry of Culture that cost more than the painting.

It feels good to help others, sometimes when you are not even aware you have done so.

Aircraft confidant

In December 1991, I interviewed in London for a new job and was returning to Jersey in the Channel Islands. The interview went well and I felt reasonably certain of an offer. After 18 rewarding years with Citibank, moving to another employer was a difficult decision.

The plane used on the London–Jersey route was small. I was sitting in the front row when a fog delay was announced. My seat mate and I struck up a conversation. I recognized him as Alan Whicker, a well-known British television personality and journalist.

As one mysteriously does on airplanes, I shared details about our difficulties integrating into life on the 45 square miles that is the island of Jersey. I mentioned that my wife was a Finn whose mother tongue was Swedish. His eyes widened and he said it might help if he introduced her to Engelbert Humperdinck's Swedish wife.

Alan continued to ask questions, and as I was answering them, I stepped out of my body to observe how a professional interviewer guided the conversation. Like an executive coach, he facilitated my decision process as we discussed my career options.

Saying goodbye to him at Jersey airport, I already knew what I would suggest to my wife when I walked in the door. I wrote to Alan a few days later to say we were moving to London.

Chance put Alan and I together that day. I was grateful to be the subject, and an observer, of a master interviewer in action. I have not forgotten how he listened intently and compassionately while gently probing my thinking without being too intrusive.

Sometimes you are fortunate to meet the right person in the right place at the right time.

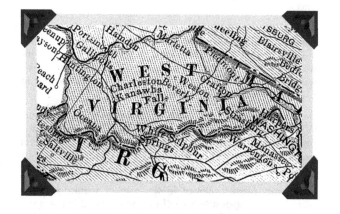

Helping hand

In April 1979, I had a perfect day.

I was a corporate banker based in New York City on an early morning flight to Charleston, West Virginia. I was seated next to a young man. He was fidgeting with an envelope, visibly nervous. Talking to him to ease his tension, I learned he had recently enlisted and was holding orders to report to his first posting at the US Naval Base in Charleston by 1800 that day.

Taking a deep breath and knowing already that we had a problem, I grabbed the airline magazine from the seat pocket and opened it to the map section. I showed him where we would be landing in about two hours, a city in a state that was landlocked. There was no way there could be a naval station in West Virginia. I then ran my finger to Charleston, South Carolina on the east coast of the United States. As his situation became clear, he turned very pale.

I quickly informed the cabin crew about his predicament. They briefed the captain. To that airline's great credit, by the time we landed in West Virginia, they had sorted the flight connections that would get him to South Carolina to report for duty in time.

We did not exchange personal details, so I never found out whether he made it. I choose to believe he did.

There is no more uplifting feeling than being able to help someone in need.

Surprise moment

Surprising moments can happen anytime, anywhere!

In 2010, I was walking near Belarus Station in Moscow and joined a crowd at an intersection, watching a three-story building that was on fire. The approaching fire brigade sirens could be heard getting louder while the police started to cordon off the area.

Before I continue, keep the size of Moscow in mind: it covers an area of almost 1000 square miles (2500 square kilometres) and there are 12 million inhabitants.

I stood gawking with others. Just before fire engines arrived, a white car pulled up at the intersection and stopped. The driver jumped out and ran towards me. Before I could react, he hugged me and kissed me on both cheeks. Stepping back, I realized it was someone I had worked with on a project in the early 1990s, building a network of training and small business support centers across Russia. He handed me his business card and ran back to his car, pulling away just before the fire engines arrived.

According to the card, he was heading up the learning and development function of a major Russian company. Afterward, we corresponded for a while, but eventually lost touch. A recent Google search shows he is now a deputy minister.

Life offers chances to meet interesting people, and sometimes to experience wonderful moments of surprise.

The start of an action-packed day at the Ferrari factory in Maranello, Italy

A mad dash

It was June 2004. I flew into Milan's Malpensa Airport, rented a car, and picked up my *Performance at the Limit* co-authors from Milan's Linate airport. We were in Maranello, Italy, to interview Ferrari's F1 leadership team.

After a busy morning, we planned to catch afternoon flights home. But then we were invited by Ferrari's Head of Communications to eat lunch at Michael Schumacher's favorite restaurant.

Gracious hospitality, pasta and Lambrusco is not to be rushed. Well behind schedule, we offered our thanks, got into our rental car and raced to Linate Airport. I dropped my colleagues off, almost without coming to a complete stop, and now had to cover 45 miles (70 kilometres) to Malpensa Airport.

I had promised to be home for the important Finnish Midsummer holiday and I now had to drive like Michael Schumacher to catch my flight.

With just minutes to spare, I pulled into car rental return, threw my keys to the attendant and ran to the terminal. With pleas and sign language, I skipped to the head of the security queue and ran through the terminal, reaching the gate as the door was closing.

Making it on board just as the door was closing, I plopped into my seat, breathing heavily and sweating profusely. A compassionate member of the cabin crew walked towards me, raised a finger to her lips to signal that I shouldn't say anything, and handed me a can of ice-cold beer.

Maybe it was the Lambrusco, but for a short time that day, rather than just writing about F1 drivers, I felt like one.

Getting home in time, sipping a cold brew, and imagining that I had driven like an F1 driver... life felt good.

4

Communications

With Jacques de Larosière, former President of the EBRD, at the 20th anniversary celebration of the Joint Vienna Institute

Visual messaging

In the spring of 1992, I was in Basel, Switzerland attending a meeting in the austere boardroom at the Bank for International Settlements. I was representing the EBRD on a Steering Committee tasked with agreeing the governance and curriculum for a new training institute to be established in Vienna. It was to be focused on assisting the transition of former communist countries to market economies. Committee members included representatives from the International Monetary Fund, World Bank, Organization for Economic Cooperation and Development, and European Commission.

In previous meetings, conflicting corporate cultures and diverse personal styles, given our seven different nationalities, had stymied our efforts to reach agreement. Amidst more non-constructive discussions my colleague and I suggested using a facilitator to break the deadlock. This type of intervention was new to most of the people sitting at the table. After an energetic debate, it was agreed.

The facilitator met with each party independently in Washington, London, Paris, and Brussels before we gathered at an English country manor, two people per organization. We set aside five days to reach agreement.

The facilitator's first exercise involved cutting out images from magazines and, in teams, making a collage depicting a vision for the new institute. After a few cynical comments, we set to work.

During the team presentations, laughter eased tensions and led to constructive discussions. With the ice broken, the institute's curriculum and governance were designed in just three days. Plus, from an atmosphere of disharmony and distrust, enduring friendships were forged.

The Joint Vienna Institute opened in September 1992 and since then has trained over 40,000 participants.

Effective communication across cultures can be difficult – but it's worth the effort.

Interpreters

Given my international travels, I have often needed to communicate through interpreters. I learned a valuable lesson many years ago from a professor who recounted speaking through a sequential interpreter to an audience in Japan. The presentation was going well, so he decided to take a big risk in any cross-cultural setting: telling a joke.

He spoke, followed by the interpreter. This pattern continued for a while, and eventually he delivered the punchline. The interpreter spoke again, and the audience broke out in laughter.

Afterward, the professor complimented the interpreter on his skill. The interpreter said, 'Honorable Professor, while you spoke, I told the audience you were telling a joke. After you gave the punch line, I said, "The professor has now finished the joke, please laugh."'

In such situations, no matter how eloquent you think you are, the most important person in the room is your interpreter.

When possible, before presentations I brief the interpreters on my main messages and any technical jargon.

If the interpreter does not get both what I am saying and what I actually mean, the audience certainly will not.

Diversity

In 2011, I was honored to participate in the 4th Festival of Thinkers sponsored by the United Arab Emirates' Ministry of Higher Education and Scientific Research and the Higher Colleges of Technology in Abu Dhabi. Other 'Thinkers' included business leaders, government officials, academics, and even a few Nobel laureates.

The theme was 'Inspired Thinking Fresh Perspectives'. Over three days, I participated in panel discussions and round-table exchanges with the likes of a CNN news anchor, Central Bank governor, business school dean, former governor of Kentucky, and a researcher studying the brain physiology of F1 drivers.

Most importantly, 300 students from 83 universities representing 40 nations took part, discussing topics that covered global challenges and pressing social, economic, and environmental issues.

The diversity of backgrounds, in an atmosphere where everyone could share their thoughts without judgment, was key to the event's success. The enthusiasm of the students who spoke and defended their points of view was inspiring.

The recipe was simple: engaged participants expressing opinions without reservation.

If we do not appreciate the diversity, knowledge, and mindsets of the people around us, we miss out on valuable inputs.

Irony

Americans celebrate Thanksgiving in November. This is a wonderful, secular holiday when family and friends gather for a festive meal and give thanks for life's blessings.

In 1986, upon arriving in Turkey, we were asked to employ Ayşe to help in our home. With my long work hours establishing the Center for International Banking Studies (CIBS), having cajoled my wife, due to budget constraints, to volunteer her expertise to design CIBS's interiors, and with two children, we were happy to have Ayşe's support.

For our first Thanksgiving in Istanbul, we invited friends for dinner at our home and Ayşe agreed to help. Ayşe only spoke Turkish and at this time we still did not know much about her.

Visiting the local butcher with Ayşe, my wife did not know the Turkish word for 'turkey' and Ayşe was silent. So, she mimed a turkey while ordering two *büyük tavuklar*, or big chickens.

On the day, with two 'big chickens' in the oven, we heard loud popping noises. Apparently, the butcher had injected water into the birds to increase their size and as the water boiled, they were exploding.

Somehow, we managed to get pieces of the faux turkeys on the dinner table and had a wonderful celebration.

Ironically, soon after the holiday, we learned Ayşe's surname, 'Hindi,' which when translated into English is a bird known as 'turkey.'

Somehow, everything is connected. The answer to our search was there all along.

Spectrum of cultures

In 1976, I was making my first trip to visit a nationwide fast-food chain based in Kentucky. Rolling hills, horses, green grass and white picket fences made for a stark contrast to New York City.

The founder and CEO took me to the company's flagship restaurant where new food concepts were tested. I was served a sampler, which included a fried ball of corn-meal batter. Seeing my quizzical expression, he said in his Southern drawl that it was a 'hush puppy.' The only hush puppy I had known growing up north of the Mason-Dixon Line was a shoe brand.

Dessert was a small pie. He asked me whether I knew what it was. 'Sure,' I said, 'it's pecan,' saying it like 'pea-can' with emphasis on the first syllable. He laughed and said, 'That's something you urinate in! It's pe-cahn,' with emphasis on the second syllable. Who knew?

My introduction to Southern cuisine did not end there.

At day's end, I took a puddle jumper, a small aircraft that flew routes between secondary airports. Stepping into the plane, I saw an elderly gentleman seated in the front row. He had white hair, a white moustache with a goatee, and wore a distinctive, double-breasted white suit.

It was Colonel Sanders himself! It would have been hard to find a more iconic symbol of the South and its cuisine.

Food, language (both vocabulary and pronunciation) and clothing are some of the most visible symbols that represent different cultures. With air travel, one is transported from a noisy metropolis to idyllic countryside within hours.

Being able to experience a wide range of cultures, either travelling abroad or even within one's own country, is one of life's gifts.

Clear instructions

In April 1992, I was in Kiev, Ukraine, exploring how to arrange a conference for power industry executives from Ukraine, Russia, and Georgia sponsored by my new employer, the EBRD. The theme 'Alternative Energy Sources' was rather ambitious, given the Chernobyl disaster only six years earlier.

I spent the day with Ukraine's Deputy Minister of Power and Electrification, who was delighted when I selected a power plant with conference facilities near Kiev for the venue, rather than a Kiev hotel. We bonded over lunch when I matched him shot for shot over a bottle of vodka.

Back in Kiev, he offered me a city tour, but that was cancelled when there was not enough petrol for the car. Rather embarrassed, he promised me a tour when I returned.

True to his word, I joined other delegates on a bus tour of Kiev before heading to the conference venue. Proudly pointing to a cameraman using perhaps their first video recorder, the minister promised me a record of the tour and the event's proceedings.

The conference opened that evening with a banquet. The next day, the sessions went well. At its conclusion, I was ceremoniously handed the video to watch when I got home.

Once in our house, I promised my wife a tour of Kiev's churches and monuments with highlights from the conference. The video started and for 60 minutes the only images on the screen were of me. Me walking, me smiling, me eating, and me listening to speakers. Not a single tourist site was included, nor much about anyone else participating in the event. We had to wonder what instructions the cameraman had been given.

Clear communication, especially when giving instructions, is everything.

5

Cultural encounters

Maintaining traditions

Dubai, in the United Arab Emirates, has become a major business and tourist destination. Glistening skyscrapers line the main thoroughfare, Sheikh Zayed Road, but it did not look like that when I first visited in 1984. Driving from Dubai's airport to the Jebel Ali Hotel, only a few buildings were visible, and the landscape was largely flat and barren.

I was attending a one-week seminar on marketing financial services. It was an intense program, and we were thrilled to get an afternoon off. We haggled and bought souvenirs at the *souq*, then visited something unique for us all: camel races.

We sat in the grandstand under a large canopy and sipped coffee while the camels were paraded in front of us. Small boys were seated on the camels as jockeys. Their trousers had Velcro patches sewn on the bottom, attaching them to blankets on the camels' backs so they would not fall off.

The start of the race took place in front of us, but as the oval track was 10 kilometres long, we watched most of the race on televisions located at our seats. Camel owners cheered their entries onward, chasing them in their cars while driving on a road just outside the track's fenced boundary.

In the shadow of the world's tallest building, Dubai has become a glitzy tourist destination with beaches, indoor skiing, water parks and so much more. You can still attend camel races. One change is that child jockeys have been banned since 2002, replaced by small box-like robots placed on top of the camel's humps.

Dubai looks and feels dramatically different since 1984, but a pastime that is believed to have derived from the seventh century has been updated and preserved.

As much around us changes, it is wonderful to see cultural traditions maintained.

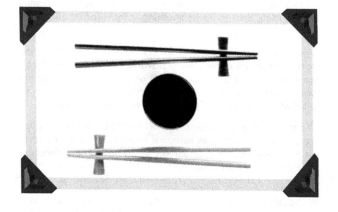

Cultural awareness

In 2006, I was in the lobby of a Riyadh hotel, awaiting the arrival of a high-ranking Saudi Arabian Prince, closely related to the King. I was there to witness a contract signing for consulting work our firm was doing for one of his investment projects.

We met the Prince at the entrance as he exited his Bentley and pictures were taken of our group in the lobby. We were then escorted to dinner — somewhat surprisingly to me, in the hotel's teppanyaki restaurant, a favorite of his. We were seated on high stools at the grill's counter, the Prince on my right and our interpreter to my left. We sat facing the chef, who put on an impressive knife-tossing display while shrimp, chicken and vegetables sizzled on the grill.

As the portions of food were cooked, the chef placed them on our plates to be eaten with chopsticks. I am very capable with chopsticks, but I am also left-handed. Just before taking up my first morsel of shrimp, I recalled that one should never eat food with the left hand in this part of the world. I tried manipulating the chopsticks in my right hand, but I was dropping most items in my lap while trying to maintain a conversation with the Prince.

This went on for a bit until the chef, noticing my dilemma, handed me a fork.

Working in cultures different from our own, it is very important to understand local ways of doing things. A cultural faux pas might at best be embarrassing. At worst, there is a risk of insulting your host.

Go with the flow

In May 1993, I was visiting Perm, Russia in the Ural Mountains. During the Cold War, it was a center of military manufacturing that was being converted to making household machines such as refrigerators. I was meeting an entrepreneur who had transformed his farm collective into privatized businesses. After seeing his property, beehives, and caged bear, it was time to eat.

His colleagues joined us for *shashlik* and a copious amount of vodka was consumed. There was nothing unusual in that, but then the empty bottles were set on bales of hay and firearms appeared. My new friends could not walk in straight lines, but they took their shots while I strategically positioned myself behind anyone holding a rifle.

After target practice, my host invited me for *bastu* in a sauna that he had built by hand. My Finnish experiences in sauna had not prepared me for his rubbing honey, collected from his own beehives, on my back and arms. I was obliged to do the same for him. It was not what I had signed up for, but we bonded.

So much so, in fact, that upon my departure he offered me a generous gift, a large wooden moose head that he had carved himself. I was touched but had to think fast to gracefully not accept it. I told him it was 'too big to fit in the plane's overhead bin and too fragile for checking in.' The excuse worked without hurting his feelings.

In one's travel, be open to new adventures... but make sure to stand behind anyone holding a loaded firearm.

VIP travel

At the 2012 London Olympics, special 'Games Lanes' were created on roadways across the city for athletes and officials to avoid traffic jams. They were also called 'Zil Lanes', after lanes in Moscow reserved for senior officials of the Soviet Union who were travelling in their black Zil limousines.

As a regular visitor to Moscow during the 1990s, traffic jams were becoming more and more common, but Zil Lanes still existed. I wondered who sat in the cars speeding past and how it must feel to drive non-stop across the city.

In September 1994, at the end of a very busy week, my meeting was running late. I was concerned that I would miss my flight to London.

I was then introduced to Alexei, a sturdy-looking man wearing a black leather coat, who was standing near the door. He was a policeman who, when off duty, was a driver and bodyguard. Soon after, I was sitting in the front seat of Alexei's police car, lights flashing and siren blaring.

Yes, we were driving to the airport in the Zil Lane!

After a high-speed journey, Alexei pulled up in front of the departure terminal and, flashing his badge, escorted me to the front of the passport control queue.

This was a rare and special opportunity to experience what it was like to be a VIP in the Soviet Union.

This was an unusual and maybe elitist experience, but it made me realize that if the opportunity arises to step back in time and see things the way generations before us have seen them, we should grab it.

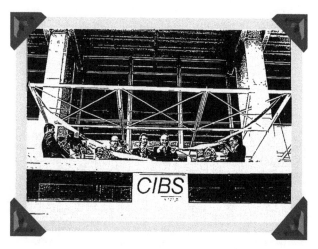

Deputy Prime Minister of Turkey, Kaya Erdem, cutting the ribbon at the opening ceremony of CIBS in Istanbul

Keeping faith

When working in countries undergoing transition, one learns that planning is important – but things are still sometimes out of your control.

It was spring 1987, and after nine months of reconstruction and refurbishment we were feverishly preparing for opening ceremonies at the Center for International Banking Studies in Istanbul (CIBS). Hundreds of dignitaries and banking executives were expected to attend. The Turkish Deputy Prime Minister would perform the ribbon-cutting honors.

The day before the event, my main concern was a dusty, pot-holed, single-lane road from the main highway to CIBS's location on the shore of the Marmara Sea. Months petitioning local authorities failed to get the road paved or improved.

We considered contingency plans to bring senior officials and the press to CIBS from downtown Istanbul by boat, but my Turkish colleagues kept saying '*Inshallah*,' it will work out. The night before the opening, I had visions of traffic jams and unhappy guests.

Arriving before dawn on opening day, I saw a fleet of bulldozers and trucks laying a two-lane bed of seamless tarmac leading to the Institute. By late morning, our new road was complete.

A parade of cars arrived for the opening on schedule, albeit driving on a soft and steamy road.

Planning is important, but sometimes one must just have faith that everything will work out.

6

Business
perspectives

Views of CIBS taken from the same spot 18 years apart

Constant change

In March 2007, I delivered a *Performance at the Limit* event for 250 people in Istanbul at a conference center overlooking the Bosporus, where I spoke about business lessons that can be learned from observing how Formula 1 racing teams operate.

I started the session by highlighting that 'Change is the Only Constant': recounting that 20 years earlier, I had been seconded from Citibank to the Central Bank of Turkey to design, build and manage the Center for International Banking Studies. I had been tasked with developing the capabilities of Turkey's future bankers. After nine intensive months of renovating a six-story hotel on the Marmara Sea, we turned it into a world-class teaching facility. It was an incredible marshalling of energy and resources by my team and partners in a challenging environment.

After leaving Turkey in 1988, I visited the site again in 2004, only to discover that landfill and a coastal highway had taken over the beach and a medical facility had been erected around the main building.

At the time of writing, the world is working through the challenges posed by the global COVID-19 pandemic. We know the world will look, and people will behave, differently from now on. But it is also true that change in perhaps other, unforeseen ways will have occurred as well.

Despite steady change, certain key factors for business success will remain constant: clarity of purpose, teamwork, and continual learning.

Fraud

In June 2020, I was reading about a $2.2 billion accounting scandal at a German company, involving fake transactions, inflated profits, and vague replies to inquiries.

I taught many sessions about corporate fraud to bankers. Learning from case studies, and examining the failures or misjudgment of others, should in theory help prevent the same mistakes being made in future.

In the 1980s, my cases included a European laughing gas manufacturer (you read that correctly), a Mexican coffee trader, and a US insurance business (about which the BBC made an entertaining film, *The Billion Dollar Bubble*). All had in common a strong, egotistical leader, a few other executives co-opted into the scheme, and efforts to mislead investigators. Think Enron or Bernie Madoff in more recent times.

While compliance functions in banks have grown substantially and accounting firms have supposedly learned from prior audit failures, large-scale fraud still occurs. I am reminded of some advice a senior banker shared after one of my sessions: 'When a man with experience meets a man with money; the man with experience gets the money, and the man with money gets an experience.'

As both personal and business financial affairs move to digital and cloud-based operations, we must rely more and more on people and systems tasked with fraud prevention to keep us and our investments safe.

Cover of Mandarin Chinese edition of Performance at the Limit: Business Lessons from Formula 1 Racing, published in 2019

Circle of life

It is November 1988 in Beijing. I am sitting in an unheated room, wearing my overcoat and holding a mug of hot tea to keep my hands warm. I had been hired by the United Nations Development Program (UNDP) to advise the People's Bank of China (PBC) on how to establish a financial training center for the country's bankers.

Over eight days I spoke about how to create a bankers' training institution. We stopped only to change the tapes that were recording our discussion. I delivered a written summary and departed.

In 2008, at an Austrian Ministry of Finance reception in Vienna, I exchanged cards with a PBC representative. I recounted my experience of 20 years earlier. I offhandedly said, 'If only I had those tape recordings, I could write a book on the subject.' I thought nothing more of it.

Four weeks later, my phone rang and a voice said, 'The People's Bank of China cannot find your video tapes.' After a moment of surprise and realizing the reason for the call, I replied, 'They were audio tapes, but thank you for the effort.'

Two weeks later, my phone rang again. 'Apologies, Mr. Ken, we cannot find your audio tapes,' and then with huge understatement, 'We are sorry, but much has changed in China over the past 20 years.'

In 2012, Tsinghua University in Beijing created a School of Finance in partnership with the People's Bank of China. Then, in 2019, the same university published a Mandarin Chinese edition of my book, *Performance at the Limit*. To mark the release of the book, I was scheduled to speak in Beijing at Tsinghua University in February 2020. Of course, that did not happen due to the global Covid-19 pandemic.

Life sometimes comes full circle, and maybe it still will.

Ideas and money

George Soros, Hungarian-born American billionaire investor and philanthropist, turned 90 years old in August 2020.

In 1992, after joining the EBRD, we were developing a strategy for expanding business education in former communist countries that required sources of funding. Various government support programs existed but Soros had already put his own money into training institutions in certain countries.

Having a few years earlier advised, pro bono, a start-up business school in Budapest funded by Soros, I was fortunate to get a breakfast meeting with him in London on September 17.

A butler opened the door and gestured to the breakfast room. However, before entering I noticed a credenza in the hallway covered with the morning newspapers. All had headlines along the lines of, 'Soros breaks Bank of England, makes $1 billion in one day.'

Moments later, the broadly smiling man himself came down the stairs. At breakfast we discussed institution building and training needs in transition countries.

His parting words were, 'I will succeed, but you may not. We both have great ideas – however, I have money and you don't!'

In 2012, Soros spoke at a conference in Helsinki. Afterwards, I reintroduced myself. I reminded him of that morning, 20 years earlier, when he had walked down the stairs wearing the 'biggest sh*t-eating grin ever.' He laughed out loud!

I congratulated him on his work supporting transition economies. I also shared the contributions the EBRD had made, even while we constantly searched for financial support.

Money does not start an idea; however, an idea – the currency of change – can start the flow of money.

Old is new

In 2005 I met a friend who worked for my former employer. He had just completed a train-the-trainer course for a selling skills program. He enthusiastically showed me the professionally packaged teaching manuals and participant materials. He explained that the organization had paid $1 million for this course, which was tailored to the banking industry.

I asked him to wait a moment and disappeared into my office.

Upon returning, I placed a binder on the table next to his. It was a program I had taught at that same company 20 years earlier. We leafed through the two binders page by page. They were identical. Same case studies, same exercises and same lessons.

My former employer had (re)purchased a program it had commissioned and bought two decades before, from the same vendor. I did not know for sure, but I suggested that the company had probably already owned the usage rights to that course and its materials.

I am sometimes surprised how short corporate institutional memory can be. This has been exacerbated by increased turnover due to the Volatile, Uncertain, Complex, Ambiguous (VUCA) world and the way the unwritten loyalty contract between company and employee has drastically changed over time.

There's nothing new under the sun.

Technology and behaviors

In 2000, I delivered several seminars using an excellent computer-based business simulation. The one-week course was designed to build business acumen and teamwork. The client was the market leader in mobile technology at the time. The venue was the five-star Chateau du Lac hotel, 20 kilometres south of Brussels.

All the participants were using a new product that allowed anyone, anywhere to use a mobile phone to access internet and email. We take this for granted now, but at the time it was a unique capability. It was my first encounter trying to establish proper classroom etiquette for the use of such devices without disrupting the seminar's flow and maintaining the attention of participants.

One program, in June, stands out from the rest for a reason that has nothing to do with the course itself. At that time, Belgium and the Netherlands were co-hosting the Euro 2000 football tournament, and the French National team was staying at our hotel.

I sat in the lobby as often as I could, watching the likes of Deschamps, Pirés, Vieira, Zidane, Anelka, Desailly, Blanc, and Barthez juggling and kicking balls back and forth while waiting to catch their bus. It was a great show!

If this happened today, I wonder whether – like my course participants who were so engaged with their new devices – they would only be looking at their mobile phones. Also, I could have got some great selfies.

With the adoption of new technologies – devices, software, and apps – our behaviors have also changed. It has affected how we communicate, interact, and work. As with all such developments, the results have been both positive and negative.

Keep it simple

Growing up in New York, Pasternak was just a surname like many others in an environment made up from diverse ancestry. Moving to Europe in 1980, my family background was of greater interest to people I met, but nothing compared with when I visited the Soviet Union for the first time in 1984. Boris Pasternak – poet and Nobel Prize Laureate – had died in 1960, but he remained a controversial figure.

Both entering and leaving Leningrad Airport, I waited an eternity as a stern looking immigration officer scrutinized my passport. Then, in 1986, my wife and I visited Moscow. We are in no doubt that our hotel room was searched often. And when we spoke with the babushka keeping watch over our hotel floor, she was suspiciously knowledgeable of our whereabouts.

Traveling throughout Russia from 1992 to 1999, I do not recall experiencing any problems; however, I do remember a 15-hour train journey from Moscow to Minsk in 1994.

Before boarding the train, my Russian colleague pulled me aside and whispered, 'Do not show anyone your American passport and do not speak English, unless we are alone in the cabin.' My imagination drifted to countless espionage films.

In fact, it was nothing so exciting or intriguing. By using my Russian-sounding surname, they had bought a domestic train ticket that was much less expensive than buying one at the price charged for foreigners.

It's good to remember Occam's Razor: the simplest solution is almost always the best.

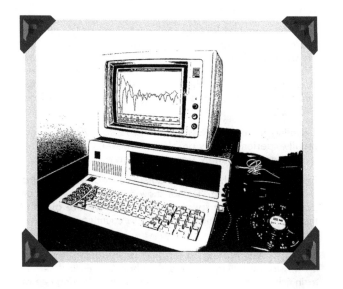

Points of view

In the early 1980s, the potential uses of personal computers were only just being discovered. A revolution in electronic banking services was coming and my financial institution took a lead in this change.

In 1984, I attended a meeting of corporate banking colleagues in Vienna. The conference focused on this new technology and how to sell our services to corporate clients.

One experience at the event left a lasting impression.

Three journalists interviewed our most knowledgeable and experienced salesperson in front of us all. After 30 minutes, the journalists left the room. We were then instructed to write a headline that, based on the interview, would appear in tomorrow's newspaper. Typical examples we suggested were:

'Citibank wires the world!'

'Citibank forging new frontiers in banking services!'

'Technology bringing great advantages to business!'

The journalists returned and shared their proposed headlines.

'Facing competitive difficulties, Citibank reaching for new electronic products!'

'Citibank making big financial bet on untried, expensive technology!'

'Are companies ready to give control of their money to a computer?'

What a wake-up call. I learned an important life lesson that day.

The story you tell, versus how it may be perceived by others, can be two or more different things.

Zafer, my wife Harriet, and our white Mercedes

Verify

When we arrived in Istanbul in 1986, my general manager position afforded me a driver. Zafer Bey was always well dressed, on time, and kept me safe in sometimes chaotic driving situations.

I bought a white Mercedes 200 from a departing expat and gave the keys to Zafer. I instructed him to take responsibility for the car, and told him to make sure we always had petrol, to keep it clean, and to have the proper maintenance done.

He spoke no English, but with my improving Turkish we were usually clear on where we were going. He never let me down. The car was immaculate and in excellent working condition.

When we left Istanbul, we had the car transported by lorry to Brussels. With my heavy travel schedule, my wife took responsibility for it. And that brought her to the Mercedes dealership for a routine maintenance service.

At some point she saw a crowd of men looking under our car's bonnet. They were pointing, chattering loudly, and even laughing. Finally, a mechanic said to her, 'Madam, we have never seen this before. Do you realize there is not one original Mercedes part in your engine!'

We never thought that Zafer was in any way involved in a parts replacement scheme, and believe he was duped by mechanics he may have trusted.

The lesson: always look under the bonnet. Trust but verify!

Motivation

As institution-building projects went, this was a challenging one. In the 1990s, while at the European Bank for Reconstruction and Development, we were working with development agencies from the United Kingdom, Turkey, and the European Union to establish a bank training center in Tashkent, Uzbekistan that also trained bankers from Tajikistan and Kyrgyzstan.

The CEO of the largest bank in Uzbekistan, a close advisor to President Karimov, provided crucial local support and political cover. After working together tackling difficult conversations and decisions, I was fortunate to get to know him in business meetings and on the tennis court.

He invited me with a few colleagues to inaugurate his bank's new sauna. Afterward, we gathered for a delicious banquet. As is typical during such dinners, the CEO acted as toastmaster. During the evening, he would make a toast to each guest. As is the custom, in return the guest would make a toast to him, his bank and/or his country.

I will never forget his toast to me. He said, 'Ken, together we have built an educational institution, which will enable my country to chart its own financial destiny; and that is worth more than any amount of development aid we receive from international financial institutions.'

I had the presence of mind to thank him, on behalf of our team, for all the assistance he had provided to make it happen.

An authentic thank you can be memorable, meaningful, and very motivating.

Thoughtfulness

At the end of December 2006, my wife and I arrived at Paris's De Gaulle airport to celebrate New Year's Eve, which is also her birthday.

Leaving the plane in the terminal, we walked towards the baggage claim carousel, departure gates on the right and duty-free shops on our left.

The crowd of holiday travelers shuffled along slowly, but suddenly all movement stopped.

Without any announcements, rumors grew among the growing crowd of arriving passengers. There were whispers about a bomb being found in the baggage hall.

My wife and I looked at each other and without speaking agreed that if these were to be our last moments, we would live them in style. We broke away from the crowd, walked into the nearest duty-free shop, and positioned ourselves next to the shelves with the most expensive champagne.

If a bomb were to go off, we would hopefully have enough presence of mind to grab a bottle and drink to our wonderful life.

Eventually we heard a loud bang. A short time later, the crowd continued moving forward. We learned later that the authorities had done a controlled detonation of a suspicious bag.

A bit shaken and tired, we arrived at our hotel. A dear friend had arranged for a bottle of champagne to be placed in our room to celebrate my wife's birthday. After our airport experience, it was a marvelous way to drink to life.

Thoughtful gestures are not hard to make, and they are never forgotten.

*My wife and children just after a surprising
snowstorm in Istanbul*

Be prepared

I was never a Boy Scout, but have found value in their motto, 'Be prepared.' It was especially useful when I was building and managing the Center for International Studies in Istanbul (CIBS).

At the beginning of 1987, after months of design and construction, we were ready to accept our first cohort of 30 bankers for a 14-week residential Core International Banking Program.

Months earlier, a trusted colleague advised me to invest in a large back-up generator. It represented a sizeable chunk of my budget, and I was hesitant, but had no regrets when in March 1987 Istanbul recorded 63 centimetres (25 inches) of snowfall.

As our first overseas assignment together after being married in Finland, I promised my wife we would stay in Europe. We just made it. Our apartment was in Istanbul on the European side of the Bosporus. CIBS, on the other hand was located across the bridge on the Anatolian side of the city. When the snow fell, I was at home and Istanbul came to a standstill for days.

Participants, faculty, and hotel staff – about 50 people in total – were isolated at CIBS when, inevitably, the main power was cut. However, I was grateful to receive a phone call reporting that all was well, the back-up generator had kicked in as planned, and classes were continuing. Everyone was safe and warm.

'Be prepared' is a powerful motto, and a fundamental way to approach all situations you encounter.

Glass half full

In 1983, I was a corporate banker in Helsinki. A Finnish client asked us to lead the financing of a project to build a $120 million paper mill in the United Kingdom that included an imaginative approach not used before. The company would rent, rather than buy, its machinery and the banks would guaranty payments to the leasing institutions rather than lend money directly to the company for their purchase.

It was a complex project. The mill's output would be delivered to Fleet Street newspapers, which at the time enjoyed large circulation. It would be built on a former British Steel factory site in North Wales. Raw material would come from forests in Scotland.

Twelve months of overcoming logistical, financial, and legal obstacles followed. Getting the project finance in place was a triumph of hard work, tough negotiations, and – eventually – constructive collaboration.

The signing of the final agreement took place in front of a large audience at the Guildhall in London. I sat on the dais, afforded the honor of signing on behalf of our bank. The Master of Ceremonies was our managing director and he asked me to prepare his remarks.

He started by asking, 'What is the difference between a pessimist and an optimist?' Thankfully, his answer was met with a round of applause.

> A pessimist sees a difficulty in every opportunity. An optimist sees an opportunity in every difficulty. The fact that we are all here today indicates that we are most definitely optimists.

We can choose how to confront adversity. A positive, glass half-full mindset leads to better problem solving and increased wellbeing.

7

Personal observations

The split

Friendly's, an 85-year-old restaurant chain in the north-east United States, filed for bankruptcy during 2020.

In 1978, I was visiting companies in the retail and restaurant industry in Massachusetts. My final call that day was on Friendly's.

I parked my rented car in front of an old wooden house for a meeting with the chief financial officer. It was not the large headquarters building I had expected. A receptionist welcomed me and said I was expected in his office on the third floor.

I started walking up an old, rickety staircase, the kind that squeaks with every step. As I turned to continue up the final flight, I heard a different, unwelcome sound. Riiiiip! The crotch of my pants split wide open along the seam. Not a small hole, but a large, gaping one.

Without many options I continued upward. I knocked on the door, entered, carefully approached his desk, and took a seat. After the meeting, the trick was how to exit. The CFO must have thought himself royalty as I smiled and slowly shuffled out backwards from his office.

As usual, I dictated my call report into a tape recorder while driving to my hotel. Recalling my predicament, I had to hit pause more often than normal to stop laughing and focus on the road.

When travelling, always pack a spare pair of trousers — or learn to sew.

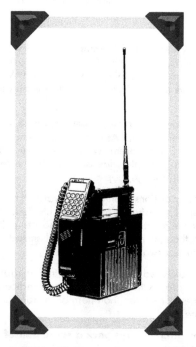

Nokia's Mobira Talkman, the state-of-the-art mobile phone at the time

Reliability

During the 1980s in Istanbul, there was no metro, no skyscrapers, and only one bridge across the Bosporus. At our apartment on any given day, our electricity, water, or landline telephone would not be working. However, we did have an always reliable Nokia Mobira Talkman. It travelled with me from my home, to my car, and into my office.

In September 1981, my wife and I were invited to an event on Büyükada, the largest of the Princes' Islands in the Marmara Sea, located just across from the Center for International Banking Studies in Istanbul that I had designed, built, and now managed. A colleague offered to arrange a boat for the trip to the island. When we walked down the pier at our beachfront location, we were aghast to see it was small, rickety, and slightly leaky.

Before boarding, seeing the condition of our boat, my wife insisted we take the Nokia Talkman with us.

As we ventured into the open sea, two huge oil tankers appeared, bearing down on us from different directions. With the tankers passing on either side of our tiny boat, we feared the worst. We started to panic as waves rose rapidly around us.

We called our children at home in Istanbul, my wife's mother in Finland, and my parents in the United States, trying to sound normal. After many stressful minutes, the tankers passed by and we continued chugging slowly to the island.

Reliability is something we look for in products we use. More broadly, it is also what we should offer to – and hopefully receive from – people in our personal and business relationships.

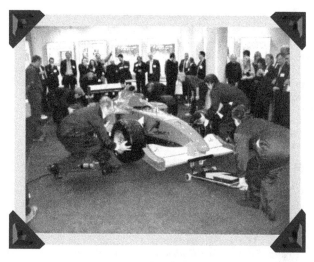

*The Pit Stop Challenge in the lobby of the IMAX Theatre,
London, during an Inspired Leaders event*

Proverbial race car

Several religious texts refer to 'a camel passing through the eye of a needle' as a metaphor for passing something through a very narrow opening. But nowhere is a Formula 1 car mentioned.

In December 2004, my *Performance at the Limit* co-authors and I produced an event at the IMAX Theatre near Waterloo Station in London for the Inspired Leaders Network.

Mark Jenkins spoke about leadership, I shared business lessons from F1, and Richard West interviewed two F1 legends: race car designer John Barnard and former Philip Morris marketing executive John Hogan.

During the evening, six people from the audience were selected to do the Pitstop Challenge: changing four tires on an F1 car that sat in the theater's lobby. Which brings me back to the metaphor.

With no wide entrance into the theater, we had to lift the car, turn it on its side, and thread it through the tiny doorway at the front. Even without an engine or filled with petrol, it was not light and was very awkward.

The Pitstop Challenge was a big hit, as was the overall event. After everyone had gone, we again struggled to pass the car through the narrow doorway and into its transport.

So next time you hear the expression 'it is easier for a camel to go through the eye of a needle than for a rich man to enter the kingdom of heaven', in addition to a camel you may now also think about a Formula 1 car.

The meaning behind this metaphor, that human beings should be less concerned with material goods and more considerate of love and respect for each other, is something worth taking to heart.

Gut feeling

In 2008, my wife and I planned a trip to India, first visiting friends in Delhi and then traveling to Mumbai. The tickets were purchased and visas were stamped in our passports. For some reason unknown to me, I bought trip cancellation insurance. As someone who travels a lot, I had never done that before, nor since.

Two weeks before our departure, I had a 'feeling' about the trip that I could not explain. We cancelled the holiday.

On November 26, 2008, terrorist attacks took place at several locations in Mumbai. This was just the time we had planned to be there.

Nine years later, we visited our son who was a visiting fellow at Oxford University. He introduced us to an American, a former CIA agent, who was participating in the same program. During our conversation, the Mumbai attacks came up. I recounted our lucky avoidance of a scary situation based merely on my 'feeling.'

He commented that feelings like that are very real and referred me to *The Gift of Fear* by Gavin de Becker. In it, the author says we can protect ourselves by learning to trust, and act on, our gut instincts.

Was not travelling to India a coincidence (luck) or synchronicity (a deeper intelligence at work)?

I will never know, but it serves to remind us that in life and business it is always important to pay attention to your gut feelings when making important decisions.

In the moment

I have never had a bucket list.

We were delivering an action learning program for a US multinational that involved meeting the participants who came from around the world three times over three months. The program usually took place in the United States, but this time we were in France, sitting in a conference room within the ornate Palace of Versailles.

Participants were organized into teams, each working on a live project that could impact the company's operations and profitability. They reported their recommendations to the CEO at the end of the third session. Team-building was of paramount importance, so we concluded the first day of the program with a team exercise designed to forge closer relationships – and have fun.

It was a scavenger hunt that required participants to work together creatively to solve problems. In the United States, it was done at a nearby museum village, but arranging it in the fabulous gardens of Versailles, which covered 800 hectares, brought a whole new dimension to the exercise.

Thus, on a lovely June afternoon in 2000, I found myself participating in an exercise while riding a bicycle around large water features, passing monumental statues, and gliding by neatly trimmed hedges. I recall stopping for a moment, looking around, and considering how fortunate I was.

For some, a bucket list may be important for pursuing life's adventures. In my experience, though, one needs only to be open to new opportunities, realize when something very special is happening, and have the presence of mind to appreciate the moment.

Home sweet home

On January 7 1991, I flew to Karachi, Pakistan to discuss privatization of a large public bank. Tensions were rising in the Middle East. We were advised to remove any personal information or indications of our employer from our baggage. Zaventem Airport in Brussels and then Frankfurt Airport were eerily deserted.

Meetings with the bank in Karachi and the US Ambassador in Lahore went well. On January 11, it was time to fly home from Karachi, once again via Frankfurt. The plane was less than half full.

Once airborne, the pilot announced that we were making an unscheduled stop in Abu Dhabi. No explanation was given. After landing, we learned our flight had been commandeered to assist the evacuation of diplomats' and multinational executives' dependants.

What had been a quiet plane was now abuzz. Women, children and crying babies were squeezed into any available seat until the flight reached capacity. Passengers talked excitedly about a likely conflict in the region and leaving behind husbands and fathers. Emotions ran high.

Unbelievably, one passenger complained for the entire seven-hour flight that he was not getting the business-class service he had paid for!

Operation Desert Storm started six days later. Like most of the world, I watched it unfold on television.

Sitting with my family, I realized that living in a safe, free country is a privilege that should never be taken for granted.

My wife and I in front of Boris Pasternak's dacha in Peredelkino, Russia

What's in a name?

The Bard asked, 'What's in a name?'

My surname is not a common one, but there are well-known Pasternaks — Hollywood producer Joe Pasternak (MGM Golden Age musicals), and singer Adele's personal trainer Harley Pasternak.

While living in London in 1994, I was sick in bed one day. My phone did not stop ringing with reporters searching for Anna Pasternak. Her book *Princess in Love*, about Princess Diana, was published that day.

Anna Pasternak is the great niece of Nobel Prize laureate Boris Pasternak. In Moscow in 1996, I became an Academician of the Russian Federation, an honor bestowed by a consortium of seven Russian universities. I had been asked whether I wanted to do anything special during the visit, so the day after the ceremony and banquet, the organizers arranged for my wife and I to visit Pasternak's *dacha* at Peredelkino.

We were dropped off at his cottage, which was not yet a working museum. There were no other visitors, only a housekeeper who, pointing at a painting of Boris on the wall, swore I looked like him. Walking through the house, his hat, coat, glasses, and other belongings were laid out as if he had just gone out for a stroll. It was a very special experience.

I may or may not be related to Boris, but I am proud to carry his surname — shared by a Hollywood icon and a fitness guru to the stars.

For some, a name carries history and maybe even responsibility, for good or bad. But for most of us, our name does not define us. We can do and be what we choose.

Lighting up

In October 2003, I was in Karachi, Pakistan working with a local bank's leadership team. Our workshop at a downtown hotel ended mid-afternoon, so the CEO invited us all for nine holes of golf and dinner at his club. I had played golf for years, but this was the first time I'd had a caddie to carry my bag.

My golf game was not very good, and I was spraying balls in all directions. Luckily, my embarrassment was lessened by the fact that my foursome partners were equally erratic. As the afternoon light began to fail, we relied on our caddies to follow and locate shots. By the time we reached the final tee, a par three, it was too dark to see the green. Two brave caddies stood on the sides of the fairway with flashlights to mark where we should aim. After we hit the ball, they used the flashlights to signal where our drives had landed.

Perhaps we suddenly found the zone, or the stars aligned, or something else happened, but remarkably our four tee shots landed in the center of the fairway next to each other.

We then looked for one caddie standing on the green, waving his flashlight, to hit our approach shots.

In the darkness, miraculously once again, all our balls landed on the green, and within easy putting distance from the hole. Walking to the green I smiled to myself; of course, we were that good.

After putting out, we celebrated with high fives and cheers. Not forgetting the role our caddies had played in 'locating' our balls in the dark, we made sure to reward them well, winking at them for their resourceful skills, especially on the final hole.

If you have the power to brighten someone's day, especially when it is dark, do it! And if someone offers assistance to you, accept it with grace and thankfulness.

Life perspective

I was in Vermont in August 1991, attending my department's offsite conference. We provided consulting services to banks in many countries around the world. After three years in Brussels, I had accepted a new assignment and was attending the conference to pass on my sales pipeline, plus contribute where I could to next year's strategy.

However, planned discussions took an unexpected turn the first morning. We were informed that the department had been sold to a financial services firm that had no experience outside the United States – or in consulting, for that matter. I was transferring out just in time. My colleagues were convinced I had inside information or a crystal ball. Neither was true.

After dinner that day, we listened to a motivational speaker. Given the uncertain and restless mood in the room, it was a tough audience, but he was an enthusiastic and entertaining performer.

One story he told was about a man who had worked hard all his life. He had bought a plot of land in a forest and visited the site every year to plan the cabin he would build when he retired. The rest of the year he dreamt about it. The man retired and a few days later he died suddenly, never getting the chance to live his dream.

It was a strong and disturbing message for a group of global road warriors, and it had a lasting impact on me.

On life's journey, get your priorities right, and be sure to stop and smell the roses along the way.

Acknowledgments

The experiences I have shared in this book could not have happened without the help and support of many people. Attempting to acknowledge them all by name risks leaving out far too many who should be included. There have been teachers, coaches, business partners, peers, clients, and friends who I have encountered over my almost 50-year career.

Many of these people impacted me in very specific ways at specific times. Whether they were involved in my life or work, they each had an impact on how effective I could be in meeting my personal and business goals. My relationships with them may have been for a time that was limited by the country in which we were living or the projects on which I was working, but memories of their advice, kindness, and consideration to me and my family have outlasted many life changes.

There is also a smaller group of people who have stayed with me throughout my life. These are special friends, work colleagues, and mentors who have provided stability and consistency. They have been touchstones to my roots and core values, even when much around me was changing.

My parents are no longer with us, but I would be seriously neglectful if I did not acknowledge the sacrifices they made to provide me with an exceptional education, the opportunities to challenge myself, and foundation of values by which I have tried to live.

Thank you to Practical Inspiration Publishing's Alison Jones for taking me and this book onboard. Her wise guidance has made a huge difference and her enthusiasm is infectious. Also, on her team, I thank Becki Bush and Judith Wise for their support. Thanks to Newgen Publishing for their creative design and editing, with special appreciation to Lizzie Evans, Sophie Robinson and Sue Jarvis. Thank you to Fons Trompenaars, René Carayol, Petri Burtsoff, and James Etheridge, who gave generously of their time to look through an early draft of the book and shared their ideas for making it a more engaging read.

Finally, my heartfelt thanks to my wife and children. We have moved many times and encountered challenging situations, and I have also spent a great deal of time on airplanes and in hotels away from home. I could not have achieved much without their unwavering support.

To Harriet, thank you for being my partner in all things — raising our children, creating our fantastic homes and being a wise and trusted adviser in overcoming so many hurdles that we have faced together.

To Charly and Alexandra, you have forged your own successful lives by embracing the many cultural influences you experienced during your formative years. I am extremely proud of you. I also thank you for your continual advice so I can stay relevant as technology and mindsets evolve over time.

Image credits